hygge (n.,

1) the Danish art of reaching a state of near-catatonic cosiness by sitting around a fire in a knitted jumper and felt slippers, scoffing cookies, downing *glygge* and (best of all) pretending to have special words for ordinary things

2) utter nonsense

First published in the United Kingdom
by Old Street Publishing, 2016

ISBN 978-1-910400-63-0

Text copyright © Ute Knut

Illustrations copyright © James Nunn

James Nunn has asserted his moral right to be identified
as the illustrator of this work in accordance with the
Copyright, Designs and Patents Act, 1988.

A catalogue record for this book is available from the British Library.

WHAT THE HYGGE!

AN A-Z OF NORDIC NONSENSE

UTE KNUT

ILLUSTRATED BY JAMES NUNN

A note on pronunciation

'*-ygge*' is spoken to rhyme with 'sugar'.*

* This is fitting, since about half of all *hygge* is a matter of stuffing one's face with home-made cookies.

aardvygge (n.)

common throughout the Nordic lands, the *aardvygge* uses its long, pig-like snout to sniff out cosy log fires, steaming mugs of *glygge* and old slippers, which it effortlessly wrests from unsuspecting victims using its sharp claws and powerful legs.

'Bah humbygge!' (excl.)

the famous cry of Ebenezer Skrygge, anti-hero of Denmark's favourite Christmas tale. Skrygge is invited to, yet declines to participate in various events of seasonal *hygge* until a sickly child and a ghost terrify him into joining in and conforming, as all good Danes surely must.

Brygge (n.)

(lit. The Bridge) Danish TV comedy genre, named after the classic series, featuring a mismatched pair of gloomy detectives in distinctive knitwear investigating a series of grisly slayings. In Denmark, where nobody is gloomy or a serial killer, this is the stuff of hilarious family entertainment and the phrase '*klygge off, Brygge, hygge, glygge*' is the local equivalent of 'Netflix, wine and chill'.

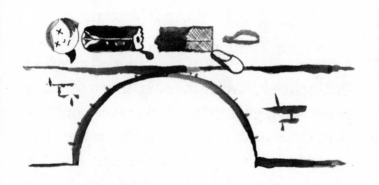

bygge (n.)

1) comfort snack best served at nose temperature over the course of a long winter evening in front of a log fire.

2) creepy crawly

See also *rygge-bygge*.

cygge (n.)

cancer-causing drug thankfully now almost unheard-of in the land of herring and foraged moss, and so heavily taxed that a single packet of *cygges* now costs more than dinner for four at Copenhagen's most acclaimed raw food restaurant.

déja-vygge (n.)

the sense that one has experienced exactly the same moment of cosy domestic *hygge* many times before and that there might, in fact, be more to life than this.

drygge (n.) (perj.)

hygge addict

dygge (n.)

tool used to work the soil in one's garden in order to provide airy and stylish living spaces for all the *bygge* therein.

eygge (n.)

ovoid shelled structure, smelly when rotten
in the state of Denmark; induces *hygge* when
served with bacon.

See also *pygge*.

ennuygge (n.)

a state of general spiritual malaise following too much *hygge*; may result in poetry, throwing oneself off a *brygge*, or both.

frygge (n.)

traditional Danish rural ice-house, made by burying blocks of ice under layers of moss, bark, herring, toadstools, plywood, etc. Now entirely obsolete in Denmark, where everyone has fridges, the *frygge* has (since its inclusion in a lavish coffee table book) proved very popular in parts of North London, where it has caused thousands of deaths from food poisoning.

fygge (n.)

1) the unique, almost palpable aroma of any room in which *hygge* is said to have taken place, comprising particles of Lego, herring, folding bicycles, plywood, smugness and Faroese knitwear.

2) (perj.) a term used to disparage those who regard *hygge* with less than 100% credulity.

'Det James Nunn – total fygge, nej?'
'Ja. Absolut.'

glygge (n.)

warm, cosy, onomatopoeic variant of booze popular in Nordic parts.

gygge (n.)

live performance of *hygge*-inducing elec-tro-trance-whale-song at which Bearded Norsemen sway gently while gazing at their felt slippers.

Heidygge, Martin (n.)

Danish philosopher who argued that the ultimate purpose of Being was sharing cinnamon cookies with friends in an exquisitely simple beach hut as the summer evenings grew shorter.

hygge

1) (n.) the Danish art of reaching a state of near-catatonic cosiness by sitting around a fire in a knitted jumper and felt slippers, scoffing cookies, downing *glygge*, and (best of all) pretending to have special words for ordinary things.

2) (n.) utter nonsense

3) (v.) to laugh all the way to the bank; often used of knitwear manufacturers at Yuletide.

'hygge-a-hydde'

the name given by the Danish press to the then Prime Minister's plan to dole out free *hygge* to disenfranchised, *hydde*-wearing youth in the hope that they would look less threatening on Copenhagen street corners if they were dressed in felt slippers. The policy was quietly dropped after thousands of well-meaning social workers were stabbed to death during its first week in operation.

Hyggenots, the (n.)

a dissenting group of proto-*hygge* practitioners forced out of France into exile in the late 17th century with nothing but an armful of logs and a zippo lighter. Many eventually settled in Denmark.

Hygge-Mygge, the (n.)

secret society of *hygge* practitioners often accused of making sure all the best Lego pieces go to fellow members.

Hygges-Boson (n.)

the smallest known particle of *hygge* that can exist in a given environment. It might be a few crumbs of cinnamon cookie on the lips of a photogenic child, or the last sunbeams of a late summer day gilding the last tufts of ginger in Grandpappi's beard, or some other bilge. Named after an almost unbearably contented seafarer of the mid-19th century.

hyggly (adj.)

really ugly

'I ygge ergo I hygge' (phil.)

the founding principle of modern Nordic philosophy. Widely considered to be too deep to translate, an approximate rendering might be 'I prefer being warm and dry therefore I avoid getting cold and wet.'

Jygge, Mick (n.)

ancient Danish rock star; gathers moss.

Klygge™ (n.)

legendary Danish eco-sandals made from reconstituted beach-waste. The company motto is *Design Before Comfort*™.

kygge (n.) (coll.)

older woman whose predatory behaviour is generally regarded as non-*hygge*.

llygge (n.)

the Welsh art of creating unpronounceable words using strings of duplicated consonants interspersed with dubious wannabe vowels, preferably around a *llwg ffyr*.

lygge (n.) (coll.)

somewhat dated term for a beautiful Danish woman

'Phwøår! That Freja Jensen is a right lygge!'
'Dream on, Maltje – she's way out of your lygge.'

is a typically confusing exchange.

mygge (n.)

1) shady character lurking in the back streets of Copenhagen armed with a Lego dagger; often dressed in a *hydde*.

2) a believer in *hygge* (see also *sygge*).

nygge (n.) (perj.)

term of abuse; never uttered in the happy, harmonious and *hyggelig* state of Denmark.

oryggeno (n.)

hardy Nordic strain of the popular Mediterranean herb; used to flavour *moose-aka*, 'Two Seasons' pizza, etc.

pygge (n.)

highly edible mammal outnumbering humans in Denmark by four to one; for some reason not as perfectly contented as the humans.

qygge (n.)

in Scrabble, the non-*hygge* feeling of competitive triumph when an unlikely combination of letters turns out to be an actual word.

rygge (n.)

1) *hygge* variant of rugby in which the players carefully set fire to the ball then sit in a circle around it singing folk songs and drinking *glygge*.

2) a style of popular music characterized by a heavy bass line, originating in Denmark during the late 1960s and popularised by *rygge* artist Bøb Mælig. Mælig's best-loved hits (such as *Recycling Song, No Wind Turbine No Cry, I Elected The Sherriff – And Even If I Didn't Elect No Deputy, I Fully Accept Her Appointment*) found fans in Jamaica, where they inspired that island's own version of *hygge, heggae*.

rygge-bygge (n.) (coll.)

one who misguidedly attempts to offset his interest in contemporary design by playing *rygge* and downing pints of *lygge* before being copiously *sygge*.

schadenfrygge (n.)

the feeling of malicious pleasure derived from witnessing the destruction of another's *hygge*, for instance by marital breakdown, natural disaster or just plain *ennuygge*.

Schrodygge, E. (n.)

Nobel-prize-winning Danish physicist who arguably took *hyyge* too far and shut his cat in a box so cosy it suffocated.

sheep-shygge (n.) (perj.)

variant of *hygge* popular in remote rural areas

smygge (n.)

critics of *hygge* point out that there's a fine line between *hygge* and *smygge*

snygge (n.)

the sound made when one comes across someone who either hasn't heard of *hygge* or who demonstrably knows far less about it than oneself.

stygge (n.)

to be called a *stygge*, and hence compared to the hero of the famous Danish children's novel *Stygge ov ar Dumppe* (*Stig of the Municipal Recycling Facility*) is a great compliment. The resourceful *stygge* volunteers to work at a recycling plant in his school holidays and sparks a design revolution that makes everyone in the town happier.

sygge (n.)

one who believes in *hygge*.

'See that fellow in the bookshop. A total sygge!'

thingummyjygge (n.)

made-up lifestyle fad so new that no one has given it a name yet. 'I was into *hygge* back when it was a *thingummyjygge*' is a popular Danish catchphrase, especially in North London.

tygge

1) (n.) a small sea-going vessel, useful for guiding vast cargo tankers full of plywood, Lego, herring, folding bicycles and lavishly illustrated coffee table books safely out of Danish waters.

2) (v.) to practise self-*hygge*

'U ygge ergo u hygge' (phil.)

the correct response at a cocktail party when the person you are talking to says '*I ygge ergo I hygge*' (see p.25). Your opposite number should then return the compliment with '*U ygge ergo u hygge*', prompting you to nod thoughtfully and say '*I ygge ergo I hygge.*' All round good *hygge*!

vygge (n.)

energy, life-force; in steep decline in Denmark since the Age of the Vikings.

wygge (n.)

Danish comfort for the cold of head.

xygge (n.)

Basque *hygge*

yygge (n.)

ancient art of exercise and meditation practised by the Vikings before they laid waste to northern England with cashmere throws and scented candles.

Zeebrygge (n.)

Belgian port; totally un-*hygge*.

zyggerat (n.)

giant terraced structure created by the Early Danes, in which rainwater was funnelled through simple turbines to provide a clean and sustainable power source for churning butter (c.f. Lurpak), slicing bacon and manufacturing knitwear on an industrial scale.

zzzzzzzzzzzzzygge (n.)

the sound a Danish family makes after a hard day's *hygge*.